THE SUMMIT

An Amazing Journey to the Blue Mountain Peak

DuBois

DuBois
P.O. Box1848, Kingston 8, Jamaica,West Indies.

i

Published by DuBois
P.O. Box 1848, Kingston 8, Jamaica, West Indies
Email address: <blackdubois@yahoo.com>
© DuBois 2007

First published 2007
ISBN 978-1-4392-2152-5
Photographs All copyright Abigail McDonáld, except for pages
4 and 19 (Alastair McDonald) and pages 48 and 49 (DuBois)
Editing and book design Jenni R. Anderson and DuBois
Cover design Delroy K. Cole
Printed and bound in the United States of America by Booksurge
Publishing

NATIONAL LIBRARY OF JAMAICA CATALOGUING-IN-PUBLICATION DATA
DuBois
The Summit: An amazing journey to the Blue Mountain Peak
/ DuBois
P. : ill. ;   cm.
Includes index
ISBN 978-976-8203-75-5 (pbk)
1.   Blue Mountains, Jamaica
2.   Jamaica - Description and travel
I. Title
917.292   dc 22
To order additional copies, please contact us.
Booksurge Publishing
www.booksurge.com
www.amazon.com

CONTENTS

CHAPTER
1

We left home in Red Hills, St Andrew at 2:00 p.m. on December 16, 2006. Destination: Blue Mountain Peak.

My family had always been fascinated by the mountains and whenever we had an opportunity we would pack our bags and head for some of the more well travelled places such as Hardwar Gap or Clydesdale Forest Reserve located at 1128 and 1753 metres above sea level respectively. We have even ventured as far away as Cinchona Botanical Gardens established in 1868 and situated at 1524 metres above sea level. The Blue Mountains provide a spectacular backdrop for these gardens which are rarely visited by the public. Primarily, Cinchona Botanical Gardens was founded for the cultivation of Assam tea and cinchona for quinine, which is extracted from the bark to fight malaria. The project failed and was subsequently abandoned. At this location we had the privilege of seeing some of Jamaica's most beautiful plants, including azaleas, rubber trees, eucalyptus, pecan, oleander, juniper, cork, oak and rhododendrons among others.

I believe that my appreciation for nature and the mountains may have started as far back as in the late 1970s when I worked at the Forestry Department in

2

Kingston as an engineer. It was during my tenure at Forestry Department that I visited the Blue and John Crow Mountain ranges and had 'mannish water' for the first time. It was an unforgettable experience.

Many Jamaicans are familiar with 'mannish water' which is a soup consisting of goat's entrails among other things. It is believed to be a kind of aphrodisiac but I think nowadays people drink it because it is a delicious soup.

My introduction to this food happened by chance because I had gone to that area with an American forestry advisor. I had recently returned from England, having spent all my adolescent years in that country, so didn't know anything about mannish water. I remember that I was having a discussion with my American colleague and we were standing close to a kerosene tin that was on a wood fire. The contents of that tin were of no importance to me because I thought that the cook, a woman immaculately attired in a well worn apron, was cooking for animals nearby. I was horrified when my colleague went over to her and asked for some of the mannish water. I certainly did not want to partake in this exercise but it turned out to be an unforgettable experience for me. I tasted the soup with the expression of someone about to drink to his own demise, but after that first taste I realized that there was no doubt about the exquisite pleasure a person could derive from the concoction. I have been drinking mannish water ever since – for its taste only!

In a strange way I have come to associate this soup with outdoor activity, especially being in the mountains.

The Blue Mountain Peak had always held a certain fascination but the dream of climbing to the Peak never materialized. My experience at Forestry along with events similar to the one described greatly influenced the idea of

Off on the journey.

making this trip to the Summit. We chose this time of year because we had been told it was best to go between December and April to avoid the hurricanes.

We were all fired up and emotionally ready for the journey.

We needed to stop at the supermarket for supplies such as water, some painkillers and energizer sports drinks, as well as tablets for Abigail to prevent motion sickness. The ever-popular 'Red Bull' energizer sports drinks were also included in our knapsacks although we were aware of the potential health risks due to its concentration of caffeine and taurine. Studies have shown that these ingredients may lead to abnormal heart rhythm and other problems. Our stop meant we didn't get on our way until about 3:00 pm. There was a most critical item that we needed but didn't have. . . a road map! We had planned to get it at a petrol station in Papine but in the interest of time, we decided to abandon the road map and throw caution to the wind . . . Blue Mountains, here we come!

We decided that Alastair would be the driver and I would be navigator. Of course, the passenger on board was Abigail.

In quick time we got to Papine, the last point before leaving the Corporate Area. Gordon Town was next and it was smooth sailing all the way. After Gordon Town, we all knew that the trip had begun in earnest.

The driving was okay but given the narrowness of the road and how winding it was, we excused, or rather, accommodated the very slow speed which the driver maintained. There were some near misses along the way.

Young beans of the famous Blue Mountain coffee.

5

For example, several oncoming vehicles did not keep to their side of the road and sometimes we were forced to steer somewhat dangerously close to the rim of precipices that appeared bottomless.

After about 45 minutes we got to the next village – Mavis Bank – which is situated at approximately 670 metres above sea level and it is relatively small but well populated area. The world famous Blue Mountain coffee comes from a gazetted zone within this area, which includes Hagley Gap, Cedar Valley, Penlyne Castle, Epping Farm, Whitfield Hall, Portland Gap among other premier coffee locations. The coffee from outside the gazetted zone is classified as lowland coffee. It is useful to note, however, that within the rank of lowland coffee there is the 'High Mountain' or 'Jamaica Prime' designa-

Ripening Blue Mountain coffee beans.

Above: *One of the many coffee depot signs.*
Below: *Coffee storage bins at Mavis Bank.*

tion that is not to be confused with Blue Mountain coffee. The Coffee Industry Board sets the standards that govern the coffee farmers and affiliates of the industry. Approximately 40 per cent of the country's estimated 12 140 hectares that are under coffee cultivation lie within the gazetted zone.

Activities at the Mavis Bank Coffee Factory.

We stopped at the Mavis Bank Police Station to ascertain directions to the Whitfield Hall Estate where we planned to launch our trek. The absence of a road map made things a little difficult so we relied on the signposts at the main villages to ensure that we were on the correct road. In some areas, to describe what we travelled on as a road would be a euphemism, as the word 'track' would be more appropriate.

At the Mavis Bank Police Station, there was a most helpful policeman who, when asked the way to Whitfield Hall, pointed to a tiny object on the top of the mountain in the distant horizon and said, 'That's where you want to go and when you get there, you'll need to go in a westerly direction to another object on top of another mountain top.' These 'objects', by the way, were barely visible to the naked eye and the obscurity caused by the mist and

The front of the Mavis Bank Police Station reflects the beauty of the surrounding environment.

setting sun didn't help either. However, we had no reason to doubt the policeman.

The landmarks to Whitfield Hall were Mavis Bank, Hagley Gap, Epping Farm and Minto. We were advised that safe driving beyond Whitfield Hall required a degree of driving skill that only people from the area seem to possess. Fortunately, we would not need to drive beyond that point.

Friendly Constable Michael Dwyer at Mavis Bank.

9

There was a sense of foreboding when I looked at the distance that would have to be travelled. Especially worrying was the fact that it was past 4:00 pm and we really needed to get to Whitfield Hall before nightfall. I then decided to take over the driving at this point, as Alastair wasn't familiar with the mountain terrain.

You might have guessed, there was a chorus from the 'penny section', singing 'Daddy, you are driving too fast!'

I replied: 'Is it better to drive slowly in total darkness or drive briskly in the twilight?'

I guessed that persuasive reasoning made them shut up. The trip was on!

The road to Hagley Gap was slippery and winding, not to mention nerve wracking. However, there was a welcome respite when we came upon a most beautiful river. This was the Yallahs River which runs between Mavis Bank and Hagley Gap. We didn't stop to bathe as time was against us – or more aptly, nightfall was coming. We

The Minto All Age School was one of the landmarks we passed on our way to Whitfield Hall.

planned to sample this beautiful river on the return leg of the journey. As I write, I am still remembering the gushing, rushing crystal flowing waters.

Above: *A beautiful face of the Yallahs River at Mavis Bank.*
Below: *Another view of the Yallahs River at Mavis Bank.*

We got to Hagley Gap where the village people addressed me as 'Officer'. I think it had something to do with my combat jacket and military style attire. Several women who were involved with the cultivation of Jamaica's only indigenous spice, the pimento, were seen sitting in groups at various points along the roadway. As I passed them, I would shout, 'What's going on?' and they would shout back 'Nuttin naw gwaan. Mek somting gwan fe we, Officer'. Generally, country folk are friendly and we expected this kind of cordiality.

It was now approaching 5 o'clock and the sun was setting. Other things were happening too. For example, a very unfriendly mist had descended on us. Fortunately, visibility was not yet zero! We could still see ahead for a few yards. We hadn't banked on what happened next!

We were on the final stretch of road approaching Whitfield Hall; in a little hamlet named Epping Farm, and while travelling up a very steep incline, a 'we've got problems' sensation enveloped us. The road was a mud track and, obviously, had had no maintenance program whatsoever over the years. The tyre tracks from vehicles had carved out gutter beds that ran parallel to each other and this resulted in a high mound in the centre that was capable of damaging the undercarriage of most vehicles, including small trucks.

Sensation was now reality as, while travelling up one of the many steep slopes, our vehicle got stuck in a mud hole and started to roll back! Rolling on a mountain slope is most definitely not an option! We did . . . and then the vehicle stopped! Our only option was to try again and hope that we wouldn't roll. We made two more unsuccessful attempts. Our vehicle, a 4-wheel drive Isuzu Bighorn, with a powerful diesel engine, started to look most inadequate on the mountain slope.

A beautiful lemon tree near Whitfield Hall Estate.

On the third attempt there was a deafening silence in the vehicle. It was becoming very clear that the road surface wouldn't hold out much longer for a fourth attempt. We simply had to do it . . . and do it now! It was a 'Do and not die' scenario that faced us. I dropped the 4-wheel drive in low-low and stepped on the accelerator. For a brief moment our hearts sank as the tyres skidded in the mud. The vehicle didn't begin to move until several seconds later and then it started to turn sideways. We didn't have any intention of going over the precipice but what was happening now made that seem like more than a remote possibility. It was a sweet sensation when we extricated ourselves from this life-threatening situation.

One view of the Whitfield Hall Estate; From the steps, you look on to the front lawn.

We arrived at Whitfield Hall Estate at about 5:30 pm. The road to get there was bad – very bad. We drove up slopes that didn't allow us to see beyond their brow until you were on them. Eventually, we became accustomed to the familiar sounds of the undercarriage rubbing on the ground as we went over them. At the gate of Whitfield Hall Estate, our faith and courage were again tested, as we had to hit the low-low transmission gears in order to transcend the last of many hurdles to get to the Whitfield Hall Estate Lodge.

The buildings on the grounds of the estate were all original structures, very old and reminiscent of a period of history when sugar was king and sugar cane plantations were many. The grounds were well kept and had a rustic charm. The friendliness of the people went far beyond the call of duty. The Blue Mountain coffee from this area is arguably the best in the world and qualitatively outranks all other crops that may be grown legally for commercial purposes.

Whitfield Hall Lodge as we saw it that night.

The trees, mainly eucalyptus and pine, were very tall and showed signs of having been around for years, far in excess of the biblical allotment given to man. Even the dogs on the property had grown accustomed to a laid-back lifestyle and couldn't care less about who we were.

Some very interesting people ran the house but the two most notable characters were the cook, Miss Lilieth, and Mr Willy who did everything else. The fireplace was beautifully ancient and he made the fire using timber logs from the estate. There was a very unusual pair of bellows, at least 50 years old, that he used to fan the fire to keep it ablaze. The smoke-stained ceiling and aged hardwood

15

Yet another view of Whitfield Hall Lodge.

floor of the dining room were signs of the times – past and present.

Mr Willy had many stories to tell about various people who had attempted the climb and had to give up because they lacked either courage or stamina. He told us that we would make it and that he was willing to bet on it. We had a look of determination in our eyes, he said.

Miss Lilieth was a very charming oversized lady. She cooked well and gave hefty servings, as 'climbers must eat plenty', she said. We ate rice and peas and chicken among other things for dinner, and drank her brand of fruit punch and . . . Blue Mountain Coffee.

Above and below: *Typical flora at Whitfield Hall Estate.*

Alastair takes a break to enjoy nature at Whitfield Hall Estate.

Another group was staying at the lodge. These ladies were student teachers with their chaperone, Miss Donna. After dinner they invited us to play Scrabble with them and we thoroughly enjoyed it. Looking back, I think they really wanted to tell us how they had failed in their attempt to make it to the Peak as well as to give us all the horror stories that they could conjure up to put us off going.

They nicknamed Alastair 'Jeg'. This came about because, after receiving a proper thrashing at Scrabble, from Donna, Nickie and Tammy, he invented a new word *jeg* that existed neither in the dictionary nor in the Scrabble reference guide. For that unfortunate 'invention' he was thereafter known as 'Jeg'. These young women, who comprised a party of about eight people, really took the Mickey out of him regarding his word artistry but all in good fun.

Father and daughter enjoying the grounds of the Whitfield Hall Estate.

Without embarrassment, they told us about their failed attempt to conquer Blue Mountain Peak. We listened to a recording of Tammy who, on her way to the 'Bust Stop' - started gasping for air as it became more rarified with the higher elevation. On the recording, she was saying that the guide told her that Portland Gap - mid point from the Lodge to the Peak - was just around the corner. She said she hiked around several bends for more than two hours, and still could not arrive at Portland Gap and the air was getting thinner by the minute. It appeared that at one point she even became delusional and was hallucinating as, she was certain that one of the signs along the way didn't read 'Portland Gap' but read instead 'Portland Gap, Whatever'.

19

DuBois admires the Whitfield Hall scenery.

At that stage, her party of eight people abandoned the trip as others in the group were having 'near death' experiences. One of them told me that she looked at her legs and they wouldn't move as all her calf muscles had shut down.

These were some of the stories that we were forced to listen to as we were all huddled around the fire in the dining room of the Lodge. The climax of the evening came when the only organist on the premises hit the keyboard of the antique pump organ in the dining room and started to play like crazy. The only songs he knew were funeral songs!

Fortunately, Abigail was spared from this encounter as right after eating, or more appropriately, overeating on chicken and rice and peas she headed off to bed in our little room. We shared two double bunk beds. Her idea turned out to be very wise, as she never learned about the

Magnficent trees at Whitfield Hall.

exploits of the infamous Jeg. Nor did she have to listen to stories of failed attempts at climbing the Peak. She had a beneficial and complete rest, albeit only for a few hours.

Our journey to the Peak would commence at 2:00 a.m. from Whitfield Hall Estate, approximately 1 524 metres above sea level to Blue Mountain Peak, 2 256 metres above sea level. Our estimated time of arrival at the Peak was Sunday morning, December 17, 2006 at 6:30 a.m. to greet the sunrise.

Our mountain guide, Everton, knocked on our cabin door at exactly 2:00 a.m. His promptness was pleasing. He had agreed to that time and kept his word. Earlier that evening I told him and Miss Lilieth, his mother, that although meeting sunrise at the Peak was our goal, it was not meant to be achieved at any cost. It was more important to get to the Peak than to expire before we got there.

Everton, our guide.

I also explained that we needed to adjust our pace in keeping with the reality of Abigail being 16 years old and female. Everton understood perfectly what my position was and nodded his head and replied, 'Yes, boss.'

There is no electricity at the lodge. Lighting is by way of gas and kerosene lamps. I am accustomed to the 'Home Sweet Home' kerosene lamps from my childhood days but this was the first time I was seeing the gas lamps. Mr Willy had an unenviable and unending job of pumping up these lamps whenever the flame died.

On one such occasion while Jeg and others were cheating one another at Scrabble, I had just commenced writing this travelogue when Mr Willy came over to me and asked my occupation. I told him that I am a company director. His response to that was: 'Aho, me could see that yuh have sense.'

Later on we got into a conversation with him and other people in the group of teachers and he was extolling the good nature of people who loved the mountains and God's creation. The girls, I supposed as a result of their being teachers, found it very funny when dear Mr Willy was referring to people who couldn't appreciate nature's beauty as 'Lunitiks'!

CHAPTER
2

We left the lodge at 2:30 a.m. The real journey had just begun!

We started out at a nice slow pace and I was thinking that I had just drunk a Red Bull and this slow pace would be 'kinda boring'. I even offered Abigail a Red Bull before leaving and, wise child, she declined. I don't remember if Alastair had one, but I took a pain killer although I wasn't feeling any pain. Alastair took one too. I suppose if a drug test had been conducted at, or before the end of the journey, Abigail would have been the only one who was drug and Red Bull free'.

The pace, I have mentioned, was slow initially but I hadn't realized then that it would not change: the pace would be constant throughout! It was the same pace uphill, downhill, over fallen trees and even severe mountain ridges. It *never* changed.

The formation behind Everton was Alastair, Abigail and I. After we travelled what seemed like the first mile Everton said 'It's at this point that we begin'. The distance travelled thus far was only a warm up. Okay, I thought, no problem.

This trail sign points the way to Portland Gap. One of the good things about our Blue Mountain experience was the signposting. Below: *This way to Jacob's Ladder.*

One of many trail signs.

However, at this point we were still at the 'pre-Jacob's Ladder' stage. Jacob's Ladder is famous among mountaineers because although hurdle-free, meaning a good trail, its steepness was unrelenting and every step seemed doubly difficult because biologically our bodies hadn't adjusted fully to doing more work with less oxygen.

By the time we got to Jacob's Ladder I had forgotten about pace many metres before because the 'heat was on!' I may have made a mistake when I drank the Red Bull because I was now experiencing rapid beating of my heart and I could hear my blood rushing through my body. I felt my chest pounding, gasping for air, perspiring like crazy and was reliving all the things I had heard from the girls at the Lodge. I panicked somewhat because I thought, how can this be happening? I am fit and full of vim and vigor! What's going on? To make matters worse the night was dark, very dark and

Typical silhouettes in the mist.

cold, and it seemed as if the heavy and dense clouds had put up a 'Not welcome here' sign for the moon. If you turned off your flashlight you would not be able to see your hand in front of your face. It was frightening!

By now I was sweating profusely. We hadn't covered any serious distance yet but I felt like someone who was *returning* from the Peak. I had no feeling of pain or anything like that, just an unusual exhaustion and constant gasping for air. I, who thought that I was the fittest one among us, was now ready to collapse from exhaustion . . . and at the start of the journey! Given the benefit of my seniority of years and wisdom, according to Mr Willy, I thought that if I could control this freak exhaustion, and work off the effect of the Red Bull, I'd be okay.

I travelled for what seemed like 100 kilometres before I

Ferns on the trail.

Above and below: *Typical variety of vegetation seen on the trail.*

was able to begin to rid myself of the 'Red Bull Effect'. Positive thinking helped me also and I recalled my thoughts en route to Whitfield Hall Estate 'Do and not die!' Also, I had to do that while remembering the stories about near death experience told by the teachers at the Lodge.

That wasn't all. As if to heighten the negative effects of those stories, we came upon some unusual objects in our path. Prostrate on the ground in our trail, about half way up Jacob's ladder were some Caucasian hikers who were unable to go forward or backward and had decided to drop where we saw them. They had covered themselves with their wet blankets and that was it for them. Busted!

My rhythm was returning and, although I could still hear myself breathing heavily, it was controlled exhalation. I was very determined to regularize 'things' so I suffered in silence. Only when I had to speak did the others realize that I was out of breath.

We got to 'Look Out' a little place that signalled the

View near Jacob's Ladder.

30

Fantastic views enroute to Portland Gap.

Above and below:*The trail was extremely dense but the beauty of the environment in each case made the going more tolerable.*

end of Jacob's Ladder. From there we would have to travel about five kilometres more to reach Portland Gap. I was back to my old self and my breathing was normalized. Good bye and good riddance, Red Bull!

This part of the journey was more forgiving. It was like selecting 'random' on a treadmill as opposed to 'hill climb'. To some extent this trail was more predictable as with every descent we were sure to meet an ascent that was at times doubly steep. We always welcomed the relative ease we got when going downhill, even if the price was having to push strenuously uphill afterwards. However, Jacob's Ladder offered no ease or rest in this regard at all. It was back-breaking uphill work all the way!

The trail to Portland Gap seemed endless and I kept on remembering the teacher at the lodge who had become delusional with the elusive sign 'Portland Gap, Whatever'. Along the way we heard some very strange night noises. Some of them were a little scary. I kept on looking back as I had taken the rear position so that just in case there were any problems I would be 'the defender'. I don't know why certain negative thoughts about security came into my mind, as it seemed as if we were all alone in the world.

There was nothing to be afraid of. However, I was still grappling with a strange uneasiness, as I would sometimes hear footsteps and the jingling of chains. When I was a small boy, I used to associate footsteps and jingling of chains with the 'rolling calf', otherwise known as duppy, demon or ghost! I thought, how strange it was that stories about poltergeists from childhood days should begin to haunt me now . . . now when I'm on a journey of epic proportions, in a less than friendly environment. To be haunted because I was harbouring negative thoughts is one thing, but to compound it with thoughts of spirits, evil or otherwise, was just too much to handle under the circumstance. These thoughts never really left my mind; they only made matters worse as the night wore on.

We arrived at Portland Gap about 4:00 a.m. This place is a Forestry Department Reserve about 1 675 metres above sea level. From what we saw in the darkness, the place was a well-kept recreation area for hikers and mountaineers. The prolific growth of ginger lilies and hydrangeas at the entrance to this reserve was welcoming. Normally, when we make a stop it's usually for no longer than 5 minutes. Longer stops would cause cooling of the body and that would slow us down. Portland Gap, even in the dark, was breathtaking. I've never in my life seen the stars so bright and so close. They were so close that you got the feeling that you could really jump and get them – literally 'like reaching for the stars'.

We stopped for about 10 minutes. This was a good stop as we sat on the wet grass and consumed bottles of water

Portland Gap directional sign.

More trail vegetation above and below.

Beautiful, high-altitude lilies.

and our energy drinks that were finishing faster than we would have liked. Our decision to leave Whitfield Hall at 2:30 am was a good one. Although it would still be cold at daybreak, it was colder at night and this slowed our rate of dehydration.

Everton, our guide, also pointed out that given our rate of travel we would not make it to the peak for sunrise; we'd get there some time after that. Hell! We thought. Who cared about making it for sunrise? We were more concerned about making it at all. However, I am prepared to wager that if we had said to him, 'Let's make it for sunrise', he would have done so.

Everton is such a phenomenal human being. He is slim of stature, dark complexioned and has the energy of a

Everton waits patiently for us.

locomotive. We never saw him out of breath, looking tired or even slightly tired. This man was the epitome of tranquility, serenity, calmness and patience – all qualities that combined to make a wonderful human being.

The hike to the Summit was nothing for him; it was just like a stroll in the mountains. I'm sure he could write many books about his adventures in the mountains. On reflection, it is true what Mr Willy told us about mountain folk: that they are good-natured people. Also if it's true that man is a product of his environment, it goes without saying that people like Miss Lilieth and others from that area are duty bound to be good natured.

Religion plays an important role in the lives of these people. Almost every other phrase was punctuated by 'God

Sheer beauty.

willing . . .' certain things would be accomplished. Religion aside, the general patois or Creole expressions were as picturesque as any language can be. The descriptions of places and names immediately create images in the mind of the listener that would not be so easily and aptly expressed in Standard English. It was also not surprising that we saw names like Lazy Man's Peak, Breezy Gully and Jacob's Ladder. Without knowing about Jacob's Ladder in the biblical context, anybody hearing the name would know that there would be a degree of difficulty involved in making the climb at Jacob's Ladder. The other names are also self-explanatory. In mountain culture, everything has a meaning: there is no redundancy in the language – spoken or unspoken. However, this is not unique to that area as,

A striking bromeliad.

indeed, the names of places in wider Jamaica such as Wait-A-Bit, Me No Sen You No Come and Big Bottom, to name a few, demonstrate the vivacity of the people and how they come alive in unison with the common language, Jamaican Creole or patois.

Although it was still very dark, this stop at Portland Gap was also good in many ways as it gave me an opportunity to reflect on some of the many exciting things that had taken place so far. The Lodge at Whitfield Hall seemed like a lifetime away. It had been established in 1776. I recall that we met John Allgrove, the current owner of the Whitfield Hall Lodge, at the Penlyne Castle–Whitfield Hall intersection after we had just extricated ourselves from a life threatening situation and were still very nervous. We shouted to him:

'How much further to Whitfield Hall?'

'Just around the corner. You have passed the worst parts already!' he replied.

It dawned on us that nowhere is far for these folks. Everywhere is just around the corner. We counted every metre and every corner and 'just around the corner' didn't come soon enough.

Portland Gap is heaven at 4:00 a.m. and I didn't want anything to spoil that now. Sometimes heightened expectations and anticipation of a destination may cause anxiety disorder syndrome. The Blue Mountain Peak was ahead of us and we had to be calm, not anxious, if we were to accomplish our goal and turn that dream into reality. Something

Tree ferns.

40

we noticed in this location that subsequently we discovered to be true generally, was that there was a most distinctive aroma from the pine and eucalyptus trees that gave the air a certain freshness that was invigorating. It was like breathing air with the fragrance of pine and eucalyptus.

Dawn was now breaking and we have never heard birds sing as sweetly in our lives. There are 200 species of birds and approximately 30 of these are endemic, more than in any other Caribbean island. Most people are familiar with the Doctor Bird but included in this list of rare beauty are Mountain Witch and Wild Pine Sergeant. They orchestrated a melody seemingly scored by a master com-

Sunrise.

poser. There are 800 endemic plants and more than 500 species of flowering plants, including the famous *Chusquea Abietifolia* which blooms once every 33 years.

We would be moving on shortly as, notwithstanding our revelry in nature's carnival of life, we had more pressing tasks ahead.

CHAPTER 3

It was now approaching 5:00 a.m., the darkness lightening, although it was still very dark. We all knew that after Portland Gap there was no turning back; this was the push for the summit, the last hurrah! Breezy Gully, which was off trail, and Lazy Man's Peak were some of the landmarks we passed between Portland Gap and the Summit. We were told that more than 90 per cent of hikers stopped at Lazy Man's Peak. They had abandoned the trip not

This way to Breezy Gully.

because of lack of will, courage or determination, but the simple lack of strength to continue.

We travelled this part of the journey in silence most of the way, the only occasional break in silence was when Alastair enquired if we were okay, or I'd say to Abigail 'everything is everything' or if she herself enquired about our well being. Every thought and action was measured and monitored. We needed to save energy in every way, as we had very little left. If you wanted to know about energy conservation you should have seen us in action! This was energy conservation taken to the limit. We were now in the thinking zone and a growing sensation that we were on the eve of a moment of a great accomplishment in our lives. This was no time for small talk; our energy reserves didn't allow it. We were on the verge of making our 'one small step'.

Qualities in my children that hadn't had the opportunity to reveal themselves came out and shone like the

On the trail.

bright stars at Portland Gap. In Alastair I saw a co-operative side and a willingness to carry the heaviest load without a murmur. Abigail's protective instinct shone like a beacon even when it put her at risk of falling. For example, every ravine we crossed or boulder we jumped, she was there with outstretched arms to assist me. There was one occasion when she turned to assist and almost stumbled when she turned around.

The trail was very narrow; one had little room for walking, let alone falling. At all times there was a precipice on one side and at other times precipices on both sides and at that elevation all precipices are bottomless. You can understand why slipping and falling were unaffordable mistakes.

Tough going.

Above and below: *Much undergrowth and many trees marked the arduous trail as we bypassed Breezy Gully.*

It's hard going for Abigail at this point.

The footsteps and jingling of chains that I mentioned earlier were coming back again. Am I gone crazy or getting delusional? Is the rarified air starving my brain of oxygen or should I look for a signpost saying 'Summit Whatever!' I shook my head but the sound didn't stop!

I asked Abigail to shout 'Time out!' as I realized she must be tired. She said that she didn't want to stop because we were going through a very dense ravine and the trail was wet and slippery. Ever so often you would see a sign that read: 'Stay on the trail, short cuts are extremely dangerous'. Immediately after the signpost you'd see an unofficial trail that just disappeared down the mountain and would have to wonder if at some stage somebody took that route and was lost for ever.

As soon as we emerged from the dense undergrowth, I shouted, 'Time out for 5 minutes!' as I needed to find out what was going on with me. Suddenly, I remembered

Trees ravaged by extreme climatic conditions.

Purely by chance, Abigail took most of the photographs that are reproduced in this book.

49

the words from a classical pop song 'I have been to Georgia, Alabama but I've never been to me'. I thought wow! This is crazy!

We sat down to make the most of the five-minute break and Abigail got very upset because I sat on a stone with my back to a precipice! I had to find a safer place to sit. It was okay for her to do the same thing as later she sat on a stone with her back to the precipice but it wasn't okay for me to do that.

Our rest break was almost over when in the distance we, not I, saw lights and heard footsteps and the jingling of chains! This time it was our conclusion that duppies were arriving – and in numbers too! Soon the poltergeists would be doing what they do best to people: scaring the hell out of them! We had nowhere to run, nowhere to

Misty sunrise.

Enchanting view.

hide! The fight or flight response was meaningless now as we could do neither. This was not even a case simply of fear of the unknown; it was hair-raising, nerve-tingling, head-raising, palm-sweating fright! Perspiration was oozing from our bodies and our nerves were no longer acting responsibly.

Our guide was some distance away so he didn't realize our predicament. We sat and waited . . .and waited.

It is said that in situations like these one should always expect the unexpected. We'd like to think that we were all rational, well thinking people and yet we were expecting some kind of ghost train to take us away! Strange how the mind works when the fear factor outweighs common sense.

Amazing beauty.

There was no ghost train. The perpetrators of the footsteps and jingling chains were a group of six Caucasian men, seemingly professional mountaineers with miner's helmets equipped with headlights. They were coming up the mountain and making some strange motivational noises. The jingling sound came from the contents of their backpacks. They passed us in silence. None spoke, and then disappeared. Were they real or not? There was no time to change our focus so we assumed that they were real even when they simply disappeared!

We were happy that the incident had passed, as we could then focus on getting to Lazy Man's Peak, which is about 150 metres below the Blue Mountain Peak.

It was approaching 6:30 a.m. and dawn was breaking. We had been hiking all night and to say that we were tired would most definitely be an understatement. The clouds seemed reachable and the fog, although not dense was

The promised land beckoned!

cause for concern. The use of flashlight was no longer necessary, the sun had risen. However, even if any persons had been at the Peak at 6:30 am, they would not have been able to see the sunrise because of the mist. The trail to this point was more or less without rain with only the occasional drizzle now and then. But now, just several metres from Lazy Man's Peak, it started to rain. The raindrops were like crystal droplets from a metering pump. This experience certainly put new meaning to 'walking in the rain'. It was truly refreshing.

Abigial, for some inexplicable reason, had left her raincoat at the Lodge. Fortunately, she had a hooded jacket. But the rain was so refreshing that when I offered her my hat she refused. I later learned that she was more concerned about my head getting wet. Alastair was fortunate to have obtained a raincoat, at the very last minute. It

53

gave him a penguin-like look but I'm sure since he was in front, he would have spared us from some of the horizontal rain droplets.

The timing of the rain was almost like divine intervention. We felt we needed a little wetting from above because very soon we'd reach Lazy Man's Peak and we would have a life altering decision to make.

Alastair boasting his 'penguin look'.

View on the way up to Lazy Man's Peak.

54

CHAPTER
4

We arrived at Lazy Man's Peak at 7:00 am and were a little disappointed with what we saw. Of course, the view was heavenly but we thought there would have been some kind of recreation area. Not so! The marker for Lazy Man's Peak was just a rock-based trail area with an unfriendly

View from Lazy Man's Peak.

56

Blue Mountain sunrise.

look. I guess that was intentional and symbolic as what would be required thereafter was sheer will and determination, fortified with strength of character. It was a foregone conclusion among us, although we never verbalized it, that if we were good enough to make it to Lazy Man's Peak, we would get to the Summit by any means necessary!

Our pulse rate increased because of what was to come. We glanced at each other knowingly and at that moment we all knew that this was it!

The final assault to conquer Blue Mountain Peak had begun.

We left Lazy Man's Peak at 7:15 am and summoned every ounce of energy our bodies possessed. We knew that we were doing something we had never done before, and would possibly never do again. We would soon be in the realms of the highest achievers for courage, determination and will. We would have conquered the highest mountain in all of the West Indies and would number among the very few that would have undergone the most hazardous, arduous and extreme Jamaican adventure. Our guide, Everton, seemed to have an in-built single speed cruise con-

This pyramidal structure marks the highest point in Jamaica.

trol that was set from the moment we left the Whitfield Hall Estate Lodge. We were now doing the last 150 metres to the Summit and there was no change in his pace. Fortunately our bags were getting lighter because we had drunk most of the liquids but our legs seemed to be getting heavier. My military-styled combat jacket that had caused the village folk at Hagley Gap address me as 'Officer' was now weighing a ton on my shoulders.

We were now climbing with our bodies slightly pitched in the forward position, and at times our chests were close

Typical Blue Mountain beauty.

to the ground as the centre of gravity of our bodies pro-pelled us forward. We had developed our own self preserva-tion strategy by not asking how much longer we had to trav-el. The last time we had asked that question our guide point-ed to the distant horizon and said 'beyond the clouds!' We decided then not to court disappointment by asking that question again. We hadn't wanted to know then, and now that we were on the final stretch, we didn't want to know now. The stress associated with every negative thought or disappointment had a debilitating effect on us and we had to avoid that at all costs.

Our pulse rate was now at the maximum; everyone was breathing heavily, barely hanging on and hoping fervently,

Blooming Peak flora.

One of the landmarks at the Blue Mountain Peak.

that the next physical step would be possible. There was this feeling of déjà vu as if the Jacob's Ladder experience was starting all over again. Fortunately, this time there was no panicking from the 'Red Bull Effect'. I had now earned the right to be at the highest point on the exhaustion scale and so too had Abigail and Alastair.

At 7:45 am in the distance we heard the very calm voice of Everton saying, 'This is it! You have reached the Peak!'

We caught up with him at the 'Welcome to Blue Mountain Peak' sign at 7:46 a.m.

Yes! We too had made it! We flung our bodies to the ground and gave thanks to the invisible hand that had guided us safely. We knew that there was no better sight

This is proof that Alastair did make it!

Mountain and sky – in total harmony.

than this in the whole wide world. It was a humbling experience to be on top of the world and seeing God's magnificent creation.

We saw the north and south coasts, the rolling Blue and John Crow Mountain ranges and more. The mist prevented us from seeing clearly the Santiago mountain range in Cuba.

At this elevation, vegetation and climatic conditions were in harmony as the plants had adapted to the cool climate. The trail passes through several distinct areas of changing vegetation, culminating in an elfin forest of stunted soapwood and redwood trees, their low canopies resulting from extreme climatic conditions. The moisture and dampness spawned a dense, shaded undergrowth of mosses, bromeliads, orchids, begonias, heliconias, lichens and lianas.

The primordial giant tree ferns, bamboos and shrubs are all fed by the many river and streams which, although

Above: *The Blue and John Crow mountains.*

beautiful, created obstacles for us to transcend. We saw plant species that were indigenous to the locale, as well as dozens of other 'nameless' trees and plants that may only be seen by those who have made this journey.

Some events cannot be fully described by words and this one, without any reservation, is one of them. Long ago we had come to the conclusion that it was not just the destination that was important . . . it was the journey that made it paramount.

Above: *Exotic tree ferns.* Below: *The Summit.*

Several things will be left unrecorded – present only in the memory. Oh, what unforgettable memories!